her

megan speece

Copyright © Megan Speece
Cover and Interior Design: Megan Speece
Cover Photo: Micah Frank
Interior Artwork: Megan Speece

All rights reserved. No part of this book may be used or reproduced in any manner whatever without written permission from the author except in the case of brief quotations embodied in critical articles and reviews.

meganspeecewrites.com

Published and printed in the United States of America.

ISBNs: 978-1-7374715-1-6, 978-1-7374715-3-0

to all the feral things

Feral Thing.. 7
When Pershephone First Whispers To Me, She Tells Me..9
Pretty Little Things......................................11
He Tells Her.. 12
When Lilith Enters My Dreams...................... 13
Remember...15
A Pawn..16
When Pandora First Appears, She Says........... 17
It's Kind of Funny.. 19
The Worth... 20
When Eve Interrupts My Reading.................. 21
Bringer of Ruin... 23
Before...24
What You Must Do...................................... 25
She will always be....................................... 27
Millennia...29
The hardest part...31
The words they use......................................32
Things they've said I'll never forget................33
In Conversation With Persephone...................35
In Conversation With Pandora...................... 37
In Conversation With Lilith........................... 39
In Conversation With Eve..............................41
I have many names..................................... 42
My name is yours.. 43
We Are All Her..44
They will call us..47
She can be... 51

Feral Thing

You feral thing. You, who outgrew the boxes they put you in, sending nails and boards flying out like shrapnel. You, who plucks every apple from every tree, and breaks open every pomegranate, letting the juice flow down your arms like their blood. You, who stole more than glances. You, who marched straight in, head held high, and demanded what was owed you. You, who grew large, not in size, but in force. You, who said loudly, over the cacophony of the people who would hold you down, that you would not be forced to be small. You, who broke all their rules for pretty little things. You, who refuses silence, who fills the room with your dreams and your ambitions. You, who rock them with your directness, your assertiveness, your bitchiness. You, who will not yield, who pushes on and on and on and on and on and

When Persephone First Whispers To Me, She Tells Me

That her mother wanted to keep her.
And she didn't know any better.
She knew the sun, and the bees, and the trees.

And then the ground opened up beneath her feet,
And she was swallowed into the darkness
She hadn't even known existed.

And she fell in love with it.
With its raw honesty.
With *his* raw honesty.

People say she
Ate the seeds
Because she wanted power.
She wanted to be Queen.

But what she wanted
Was to be his Queen.

To build a life with him.
To love him
As he loved her.

To make him happy
The way he made her.

He protected her,
Provided her with a Kingdom.
And they presided over it together.

All she ever wanted
Was to be his wife.

Pretty Little Things
Butterflies.
Hummingbirds.
Dragonflies.
Daisies.
Poppies.
Roses.
Twinkle lights.
Diamonds.
Sequins.
Glitter.
Barbie Shoes.
No me.
Not us.
Not we.
Not I.

He tells her
To be kind.
To be quiet.
To be good.

He tells her
She cannot.

She cannot
Run for office.
For she is
Too emotional.

She cannot
Fight the war.
For she is
Too weak.

She cannot
Be a leader.
For her voice
Is too shrill.

She pushes back.
Time and again,
He is proven wrong.

And yet
He tells her
He tells her
He tells her

When Lilith Enters My Dreams
She tells me not to settle
For the first man who shows interest.
She tells me that we are in control of
What we do.
Who we submit to.
If we submit at all.

She tells me that
Standing by her own worth
Is the best thing she's ever done.

And that the man
She married,
Stands by her worth too.

Remember

If they bury you,
You'll fertilize the land.
And something
Will grow out of you
That forces them to remember
What they've done.
   If they set you alight,
   Your blazes will warm
   The night and strike fear
   Into the hearts of men.
      If they put out your light,
      Then they will survive
      In darkness.
      Fearing every bump,
      Every scrape, every scuttle.
  No matter how
  They try to rid themselves
  Of you.
There you will be,
Hiding in the shadows
Of your absence.

   You cannot be destroyed.
   You simply will not allow it.

A Pawn

In the power struggle between men.

Somehow both victim and catalyst.

Our bodies used and put on the line.

For his war.

Launching his ships.

For his politics.

Granting him the golden fleece.

So he can parade us around and say

He won.

But it isn't the other man that loses. Not really.

It's us.

The victim.

The catalyst.

When Pandora First Appears, She Says

That she still loves her curiosity.
That she was never meant to
Settle down and be the good little wife.

She was meant to explore.
And learn.
And create.

Even if her greatest creation
Ever offered to the world is
Havoc.

It's kind of funny.

How she's both.

Powerless and the great ruiner.

Women and children first.

The implication there is…

She needs to be protected.

She's incapable of doing for herself.

Child-like.

Not even a full fledged person yet.

And yet…

And yet she's also the great ruiner.

The one that opened the box.
Took the pomegranate seeds.
Fled from the garden and embraced the wild.
Ate the apple.

She must be protected and looked over at all costs.

Because if you turn your back for even a moment

She'll destroy everything.

She'll do what needs doing.

The Worth
Of a woman.
It's said to be in her ability to create life.
Creating life is god-like.

But even our creation stories
Skip over the worth of a woman.

Adam is created out of the earth
Lilith, too.
No mother necessary.
No womb.

Eve is created from Adam's rib.
No woman necessary here either.
Only man.
And God

Ask and Embla
Are created from trees.
By three male gods.
No mother.
No womb.

Manu and Shatarupa
Were made when
A Male god split himself in two.
No mother.
No womb.

When Eve Interrupts My Reading

She tells me she still
Thirsts for knowledge.
That she's always seeking it.
And learning something new.

And sharing her new findings with Adam.
Who eventually forgave her.
And sees her unquenchable thirst
Not as a sin.
But as endearing.
And as something of value
That his wife provides for them.

Bringer of Ruin
Open the box.
Accept the pomegranate seeds.
Marry for love.
Grant the golden fleece.
Love your enemy.
Cut the hair.
Flee the garden.
Eat the apple.
Live the life you've been given.

Before

Before the crusades, the forced assimilation, before they stole the rites and rituals to make the conversion easier. Before they demanded for women to learn in silence and have no power over men, before we were reduced to less than we are. Before they burned us for daring to live independently. We were goddesses. And matriarchs. We were warriors, and seers, and respected leaders. And so much of that was lost. Because history is written by the winners. Our accomplishments, the respect had for us, our equality was buried beneath mountains of patriarchal and puritanical writings.

They buried us. Our importance. Our contributions. Our reality. And we wept.

Still, we weep.

But now we weep, shovels in hand, and we dig. Revealing and reveling in the truth of our histories.

What You Must Do
When they ignore you.
         And sometimes when they don't.

When they sell your ideas
         As their own.

When they diminish your value.
When they congratulate themselves
         For the work you have done.

When they try to smother you
Between their heads grown too big.

When they bury you alive
         With the weight of the trophies you
         earned them.

         You must summon
         All your strength.
         You must call on
         The power of every
         Person who has stood
         Where you are,
         Ignored, smothered, buried.
         You must awaken your darkness.
         Awaken your anger.
         Summon the monsters
         That live inside you.

         You must show them
         The hell of their own making.

She will always be

too much
too little
too pink
too dark
too soft
too hard
too smart
too dumb
too careful
too brash

too
too
too
too

(and never just enough)

Millennia
Of blame.
Of rules.
Rules broken.
Rules made.
Of being told you're too much.
Quieten yourself.
Both foul beast and demure kitten.
The woman who broke the rule.
The woman who was curious.
The woman who wanted the kingdom.
The woman who wanted to be equal.
The woman who wanted the knowledge.
The women.
The woman.
The same.
Many names.
Many stories.
One seed.
Millennia of punishment.
For one seed of man.

The hardest part

is how we've turned on each other

We hold each other down,
Stilletto to one neck,
Flats to the other.

Suffocating each other with judgement.
How could she cook for him?
Why does she wear makeup every day?

How sad it is that she's abandoned the idea of a family in order to climb the coporate ladder? She had so much potential and she squandors it with playdoh and finger paints.

She's betraying us.
She's betraying herself.

she is

she is

she is

she is

(having a hard enough time in this world without your judgement, thanks)

The words they use

bossy
shrill
bitch
(authoritative)

                        meek
                        weak
                        doormat
                        (accomodating)

arrogant
haughty
presumptuous
(confident)

                        high standards
                        perfectionist
                        over-valued
                        (knowing your worth)

emotional
irrational
hysterical
(human)

Things they've said I'll never forget

"Now I see what the problem is. It's not that you're not pretty. It's that your standards are too damn high."

(as though being pretty is the most important thing to be)

"You were such an authoritative bitch."

(because being in your early twenties and knowing what you want out of life is intimidating)

"Don't let them walk all over you... especially her."

(because holding people accountable isn't supposed to happen when you're just a little girl)

"Shut up honey, the men are talking."

(because you could not possibly hold a valid opinion about this complex topic)

(nevermind that I was just living my own values)

In Conversation With Persephone
My story is told as though I am a third party observer to all of it.
My power is taken in some form or another with every retelling.
First, my mother hid me away in a world described as perfection.
But, I will tell you, perfection doesn't exist.
The sun shining, the bees buzzing, the plants blooming always…
It's not perfection. It's unbalanced.

And then I'm snatched away by something evil, something vile.
But, finally, I saw the balance.
Where I had come from was light, and life.
And here, with him, was dark and death, and bitter loneliness.
Things I could understand.

I ate the seeds on purpose.
Call it an act of rebellion if you want.
An act of a young woman, not thinking of the consequences.

What it was, was an act of balance.
An assertion of power.
Staking my claim.

Light doesn't exist without dark.
Life doesn't exist without death.

And I wanted to relish in all of it.
And I wanted to relish in it with him.

In Conversation With Pandora
I came first. Molded of clay, and born of vengeance.
I was gifted with beauty, cunning, curiosity, and stubbornness.
And I was gifted a jar, that held unknown gifts.
And I was told that I could never open the jar.

But then I, myself, was gifted to a god.
As a wife.

I was created to belong to someone else.
Not to use my gifts, my beauty, my cunning, my curiosity, my stubbornness for myself.
But to be in service of the gods, of a man, of someone outside myself.

They will tell you that I just couldn't stymie my curiosity.
It's my fatal flaw– that which was gifted upon me.

But I will tell you, I never wanted to stifle any of my gifts.
I wanted to use them for me.

So I opened the jar, because it was what I wanted.

And thus I released evil upon the world.
They'll tell you I was scared.
That I rushed to seal the jar because I saw the evil.
But I wasn't, and I didn't.
I saved hope because it was what I needed.
I needed hope.
Because my power had been stolen.

In Conversation With Lilith
I was raised from dirt, my hand in the hand of the
man called Adam.
We were raised together, of the earth.
But Adam wanted me to submit.
To be his.

I saw us as equals.
I wanted us to belong
To each other.
When he realized that I would never be his
If he wasn't also mine,
He threw a tantrum.
And I left him.

They'll tell you I was cast out,
That god took Adam's side.
That I was meant to submit.
The stories take my power,
Reduce me to evil.

As though good and evil are
Two distinct, whole things,
Not interwoven together.
I took control of my path, my life.
I fell in love with a man who sees me as his
equal. Another who is cursed as evil.

But I know him to be kind and true to his word.
A rebel like me, someone who saw the world
In its in between places.
Those snarled roots where good and evil are
intertwined.

It is here, in those knotted patches of truth, that
we rule.

In Conversation With Eve
Here's the thing about my story.
They say I was tricked.
A serpent most foul, wrapped around that
Beautiful tree and mesmerized me.
Tricked me into taking the fruit.

They also say my creator
Is kind and forgiving.

So let me ask you,
If I was, indeed, tricked
Why then would I not be forgiven?

I was not tricked.
I'd grown bored of the perfection of the garden.
It seemed to me, incomplete.
I yearned to know more.
To find the pieces I knew in my heart were missing.

So I pulled that fruit from the tree
Without a second thought.
No tricks, no crying foul.

And the knowledge was
The sweetest thing
I ever tasted.

I regret nothing.

I Have Many Names.
I am also nameless.
A beautiful contradiction.
A horror story
Meant to warn the men.

My Name Is Yours
And yours is mine.
And we are all mixed up together.
In the nightmares in their minds.

We

Are

All

Her

**Pandora&
Persephone&
Lilith&
Eve**

They will calls us
Many things.
But never our names.

We will be
Ladies
  Women
    Finer sex
      Females
        Whores
          Bitches
            Sluts

                    Resist.
            Scream your name.
                  My name.
                  Our name.
            From the rooftops.

                Drown them out.
                Put our name
                In their heads,
                So they may
                Never forget.

What I've Learned From Our Little Chats
Is that we all have a place.
A path we must forge for ourselves.

And some of us will be wives,
And will be happy
In service to our families.

And some of us will be explorers,
In service to our community
Coming in the shape of discoveries.

And some of us will be
Devourers of knowledge.
Rushing from one text to the next.

And all of these things,
All of the paths we may choose,
Are valid paths.

No one else gets to tell us
What is right for us.

Not the men.
Not the women.
Not the misogynists,
Nor the feminists.

it's valid. it's valid.

She can be

Warrior
Wife
Wonderer
Wanderer
Wistful
Watchful
Wicked
Wonderful
Warm
Wintery
Wholesome
Wild
Weak
Wonderous

Exactly who and what she is. A complicated person with intricate interweavings of interests and values. And none of those things have inherent judgement-- not negative or positive. They just are. And what she does with them, who she allows herself to be, despite everyone else...

That's what matters.

Acknowledgements

This is one of those projects that was born out of random inspiration and completed in rapid fire. If you know me, you know this is how I typically work. I am struck by an idea while going about my daily life, and I am filled with an incessant need to do it now.

This intense form of hyper focus can make me difficult to live with. So my first acknowledgement must always go to my husband, who suffers from the constant whiplash of my changing interests. It should go without saying that none of the poems in this book were written as a result of interactions with him. But people will question it anwyay. I couldn't think of a better partner, cheerleader, supporter, provider, or protector, Kori. Thank you for everything.

Thanks, as well, to Maxine who suffered through mulitple messages a day about my poetry, and my many irons in the fire.

Thanks to Teresa and Misty, who didn't even know I was working on this, but keep me sane with group activities outside of the house. You re wonderful adventure buddies and I love you both.

Thanks to everyone who has been patiently waiting for me to write something--anything--for almost three years. Nothing is more frustrating to someone with ADHD than our inability to force ourselves into hyperfocus. Maybe someday I'll learn that trick and you'll get more spooky ghost stories. (I am working on it.)

About The Author

Megan is a great lover of horror and thriller, and writes spooky stories of all sizes, with a focus on ghosts, uncomfortable truths, and strong female characters.

She lives in Washington with her husband and two dogs and spends most of her time reading, going to movies, and reffing roller derby with her friends.

To find more by and about Megan, visit meganspeecewrites.com

www.ingramcontent.com/pod-product-compliance
Lightning Source LLC
Chambersburg PA
CBHW041724070526
44585CB00006B/139